Making Disciples through Small Groups

Why Small Groups Are Essential for Today

Laurence Singlehurst
Director, Cell UK

Trevor Withers
Team Leader, Cell UK

GROVE BOOKS LIMITED
RIDLEY HALL RD CAMBRIDGE CB3 9HU

Contents

Church Mission Society supports the Grove Mission and Evangelism Series
At Church Mission Society, we believe that every Christian is called to join in God's mission, whether that means crossing the street or crossing continents, and we want to set people free to put that call into action.

First Impression November 2021
ISSN 2399-6536
ISBN 978 1 78827 203 2

Introduction

1

This booklet seeks to highlight the valuable part that small groups play in enabling Christian discipleship, and particularly, in effective evangelism through their members. It is written jointly by Laurence Singlehurst and Trevor Withers. The chapter headings reflect this.

With a loss of confidence in authority figures in recent decades, the need for peer influence has been increasingly necessary, especially when it comes to mission and discipleship.

The recent challenge of the pandemic has also highlighted the need for effective small groups: during the pandemic central church resources were no longer available to support church members in their missional activities. Many of these activities that had been corporate needed to be done by individuals.

This has raised the question in many churches of how to equip people to grow in their discipleship and engagement missionally. We believe that small groups have always done both of these things very effectively: each believer develops their spiritual life and outreach, supported by their small group.

Let us be encouraged to think, strategize and plan in both the large corporate setting and in the small group setting. When these two work together the heart of our churches will beat strongly, bringing life to many.

We have written this book to reinspire you if you already have groups in your church and feel they are a bit flat. You may just have a few groups and are looking for ways to get more up and running. Perhaps you do not have any small groups and are wondering how to start. You might be sceptical about groups, having tried them in the past and found them wanting in some way. Wherever you find yourself, our prayer is that the following pages will give you fresh insight and renewed vision, along with practical application, to create holistic small groups with a missional heartbeat.

2

Laurence Singlehurst

The Small Group Movement

Interest in small groups from the early church to the current moment has tended to come and go, even though Scripture records the church meeting in larger gatherings, in the temple, and small groups, in people's houses (for example Acts 2.42–47). We see the 'one another's' of Scripture—over fifty of these statements in total—including 'teach and admonish one another,' (Col 3.16) or 'spur one another on toward love and good deeds' (Heb 10.24). These verses contain an encouragement for each person to bring a contribution. All of this took place in people's houses in small groups. However, over the centuries church has more often than not formed itself round the Sunday celebrations; small groups have come in and out of fashion.

What has changed? What would make small groups really important for us today and something that churches should reconsider and re-energize? The answer is the realization that the church must mobilize the laity, the ordinary church member. In the New Testament we see this power of participation, these wonderful 'one another's' which are awkward to do in a larger Sunday gathering. They are, however, the bread and butter of a small group. This is what a good small group does—it encourages participation and it gives space for contribution. The members' confidence grows; they realize that they are there to be salt and light and make a difference in their communities, to share their testimony. This must be the future—an energized body of Christ, every member playing a part.

So, in this second chapter I look at four things—change, connectedness, central church and the equipping of church members. The four compelling ideas revitalize our focus on small groups.

Change

We have just been through a pandemic that has created change across the world on an unparalleled basis. The norms of our society and our freedoms have been challenged. Many people have worked from home, which just over a year ago would have seemed impossible. We have discovered the power of the online world, using it for work relationships, church, shopping and many other aspects of our lives. Historically, missiologists, who look at missional trends, know that change brings openness and, in some cases, spiritual openness. Many of us might have experienced this on a personal basis. A crisis or a change in location has made us rethink our norms.

Change does not just have an impact on us as individuals. There are also times when whole cultures go through change and that change brings openness, sometimes to positive things, sometimes to negative things. An example of this would be after the Second World War, which caused a major shakeup of our Western culture: traditional values were beginning to change. One part of that change was a move away from church, but another part was through the Billy Graham movement and his worldwide preaching that resulted in a renewed interest in Christianity.

Following the pandemic there is evidence in our own nation that people have shown a new interest in reading the Bible. Alongside watching church online, this change is causing spiritual openness. As the Archbishop of York, Stephen Cottrell, said in an article from the Church of England 'Many churches report that they have more people participating in their online services than used to meet in person. Of course, I hope these new online worshippers will join us in person one day. But even if they don't, we must carry on nurturing these online communities and seeing it as a way of reaching out to new people and building new communities of faith.'[1]

Connectedness

Even more interesting, and to the surprise of us all, many of us have got to know our neighbours in a whole new way. Many more streets and cul-de-sacs now have a WhatsApp group. The Queen said in her VE day commemorative speech, 'But our streets are not empty; they are filled with the love and the care that we have for each other.'[2] She was talking about how neighbours were caring for one another in the pandemic, helping one another and creating a new community. This is really interesting from a missional perspective. We know that in the eighteenth-century revivals, people worked where they lived and lived where they worked. This connectedness was a real benefit to people as they saw the reality of Christianity being lived out in changed lives. This was attractive—others came to faith as a result and believed for themselves. What has happened today and will be a trend for the future is that a good number of people will work from home either in a part- or full-time capacity. This will perhaps give us a greater connectedness to our neighbours.

Central Church

Over the time of the pandemic, we experienced the shock of not meeting together on Sundays in person. We have discovered the power of the internet as church has beamed into our houses. This has had a positive effect in that many people who would not normally come to church experienced church via the medium of the internet. But we have also lost many of the ways people would historically come to faith, for example, meeting a Christian and being invited to a Sunday service, or meeting the church through a caring project.

Equipping Church Members

What we learn is this—the frontline of church is its people; it is our church members who are the friends and neighbours. Many church leaders are commenting that we have placed too many eggs in our Sunday church basket. We need to consider urgently how we equip church members and inspire them to step into the opportunity we now have before us. We, at Cell UK, know from over twenty years of working with small groups that groups which facilitate their members to speak and participate give a sense that God can use individuals. Small groups that equip people specifically in the missional arena have been effective in mobilizing their church members to have many friends, to be a good neighbour and to help others on the journey to faith. So, we believe that this is the moment for small groups as well as church on Sunday. Together this makes a dynamic partnership between the big and the small that could see many more people come to faith in the years ahead.

This is the moment for small groups as well as church on Sunday

These small groups could meet either online or face to face. Many church leaders are talking about a hybrid church where Sunday worship could be available face to face or through the internet, and that could be true of small groups too. Many churches have run effective online small groups through the pandemic. Some of these have chosen to use a simpler structure called the 3Ps: Presence, Pressure and Purpose. This involves an act of presence maybe around a verse of Scripture, an opportunity to share an area of pressure or praise, and then finally for us to pray for each other around our purpose and seeing the kingdom come in the different areas of our lives. The group can also be involved in what the central church is doing, for example, opportunities to bring people to guest services, Christmas services, *Alpha* and Easter. So, the future might look like some small groups meeting face to face, some meeting online and some doing both.

Over the last twenty years or so one of the strengths of small groups is that they can work in diverse ethnic backgrounds. There are many churches with people from wealthy and poor backgrounds and different ethnicities and that seems to work with very little problem. For about twenty years, *Fusion* have successfully run small groups in university settings with university students and have shown that small groups work very well for young adults. So, we can have confidence in the opportunities that lie ahead of us as we work with small groups across any demographic.

Of course, there will be challenges but there can be flexibility for the various groups that we have in our churches across the UK. Let us look now at why small groups are increasingly vital in today's world.

3

Trevor Withers

The Future is Mobilized Church Members

As Laurence has made clear in the previous chapter, we have a wonderful opportunity, a missional moment if you like, in the aftermath of change. Jesus' last words to his followers, after their world had been turned upside down, were to encourage them; he says, 'All authority in heaven and on earth has been given to me. Therefore, go and make disciples of all nations, baptizing them in the name of the Father and of the Son and of the Holy Spirit, and teaching them to obey everything I have commanded you' (Matt 28.18–20).

The Current Context

Though familiar to many of us, these words take on a completely new meaning and emphasis in our current context. Let me explain why I think this is the case.

First, for the first time in a long time we find ourselves in the UK in a similar place to those early followers of Jesus. We are living in a multicultural society, which is very pluralistic in nature. We have moved away from the Christian moral framework that has been our heritage, but is no longer the space we live in, often described as post-Christendom. It requires us to move from maintenance to mission.[3] This, combined with our highly individualistic approach, means that connection with individuals is essential and a blanket approach to evangelism and mission is unlikely to bear much fruit.

Secondly, we live in an age where institutions and leaders are often not trusted in the way they used to be. This means that church leaders in particular have limited influence. They are unable to make the sort of mass evangelism work that may have been possible before. The person at the front is often perceived as having a hidden agenda. This leads to us doubting their sincerity and often not trusting what they say.

Thirdly, people are not as interested in whether what we say is true as much as they used to be; instead they want to know if it works. For this to be proven people have to get to know us and see how our faith works in practice. In other words, we need to walk the talk and not the other way round. This also means that each one of us needs to be living our faith out in practice.

Fourthly, everyone is starting from their own particular place, carrying their own beliefs. These are often a pick-and-mix selection of ideas, often based on life's experiences and shaped by peers' perspectives, seldom thought through and worked out, but just picked up along the way.[4] For this reason, we will need to get to know what these perspectives are and allow them to trust us enough to share them with us. As they do this, we may be able to make connections for them to the Jesus we follow.

Fifthly, there is a language barrier. The words we use about faith used to have resonance; they were in general public use and were understood. This is not the case any more. We will have to start from a very different place as we talk about the faith we have and not assume that our friends have the same vocabulary as us. We will need to look for words and metaphors that connect with them. This again takes personal one-to-one connection. For more on this, see *The Gospel Message today*.[5]

Sixthly, recent research confirms that most people who have conversations about faith that help them become followers of Jesus had these conversations with a friend. This is 44% to be precise, followed by the next highest, 18%, with family members.[6]

If you reflect on your own discovery of Jesus, you may find that a number of these are true for you. Spend a few minutes reflecting before you read on.

If you resonate with what I have just described then we need to find a way to encourage each person who is a follower of Jesus to be confident in the faith they have, and be able to share it effectively with those they are in contact with.

Growing in Faith and Action

Small groups with a missional heartbeat offer a place where each member of the group can not only grow in their own faith but also be encouraged to share that faith in both word and deed with those they spend their lives with, at home, in their local community or in the work place.

On Sundays, we are often passive observers and receivers, which is fine in one respect and necessary in larger gatherings. However, we also need places where the truth we have encountered on Sundays can be worked out, and the practice of making disciples, which is each of our callings, can be realized. The place for this is our small groups where we can have a voice, engage in discussion and practise our faith in a safe and supportive community. It is not that we do not want to apply what we have learnt, it is just that for most of us we need help from others to do this. Let me tell you a story that illustrates this.

On a day out as a young man, I was captivated by a lady who was playing a grand piano. I thought how great it would be to play the piano like her. A few years later I signed up for lessons and my dream started to have legs. Every week I practised because I knew my teacher would ask if I had done so. I made steady progress, all the time imagining that one day I would sit down and play like the lady I had heard all those years ago. However, my teacher then moved away and despite still being passionate to learn to play, I did not continue to practise once the weekly lessons stopped.

I tell you this story just to highlight what I have discovered is a common challenge for most of us. We have dreams of becoming more like Jesus, of seeing others discover him for themselves and seeing our world changed as the kingdom of God comes. However, these ideas and dreams often stay as just that because we do not have somewhere to see them come to reality. So, just as I needed a weekly lesson at the piano, we need a regular commitment to a small group. Not just any small group but one that will take an interest in our growth as a follower of Jesus, and where we can also play our part in helping others grow too. These are the small groups that we have in mind as we write this booklet and, in the coming chapters, we will paint a picture of what they look like and how they can work.

Over many years I have asked a question in different settings as a way of conducting informal research: 'What has most helped you grow as a Christian?' You might like to think about your answer to that question before you read on.

I have collected three main responses to the question, and they are as follows:

- Hard or challenging times, or being thrown in at the deep end.
- The support and encouragement of a Christian friend.
- Being part of a small group.

What is interesting about these answers is that they do not mention the main aspects of church life that we might expect. No one has ever responded by saying 'All the sermons I have heard over my lifetime' or 'The wonderful worship.' These obviously play a part, but for most people they are not the most important things that have enabled their growth. So, based on my informal research, one of the most likely places we will grow as a Christian is in a small group, where we have the support of Christian friends and the opportunity to be challenged and grow in our faith.

Overall, just over a third of people who attend church every month (36%) are part of a small group, leaving two-thirds of churchgoers (64%) who are not part of a small group.[7] Imagine the possibilities if the other two-thirds were in a small group as well.

In the following chapter Laurence gives an important wider perspective as we look at some of those who pioneered small groups, and how this transformed their culture.

Laurence Singlehurst

4

Learning from History

In the preceding chapter Trevor shared some thoughts on the importance of small groups in today's world. Now I want us to take a step back and look at two areas. First, the church as seen in the New Testament and secondly, probably the most successful small group model our nation—if not the world—has seen. This is the small group dimension of early Methodism initiated by John Wesley.

If we look at the early church in the New Testament, we have to be honest and recognize that what we get is glimpses of how the church operated. Some of what we see was out of necessity because of the context of the time, and some would have been out of choices made to follow Jesus' teaching. It is certainly not a manual or a guidebook of what the early church did, and is always open to interpretation.

As I mentioned earlier the church operated in the big and the small and interestingly we see a very participative model of church (Acts 2.42–47). Let us remind ourselves of some more of those 'one another' and 'each other' statements: we 'carry each other's burdens' (Gal 6.2) and 'When you come together, each one has a psalm, a hymn, a revelation' (1 Cor 14.26). For me there is a clear picture of everybody being involved, which would not have happened in a big meeting, but it is the picture of a house church, a small-group meeting.

Small Groups in Methodism

John Wesley would have seen some of this in the New Testament. He was part of a small group in Oxford; he looked at the Moravians and then began to experiment with his own small group ideas.

What was England like in the 1730s? England had gone through a time of deep spirituality during the Puritan movement and the Civil War. The new king, Charles II, opened up a new era when the strong Christian values of the Puritan period were suppressed, and a new hedonism emerged. This was seen in a booming gin culture; it is estimated that by 1730 there were 7,000 gin shops producing 10 million gallons of gin each year. Alongside the gin, London became the vice capital of Europe. It is said that

In the 1730s a new hedonism emerged

one in eight women was a prostitute, and alongside this was a huge entertainment industry. Slowly but surely money was growing in its importance.

Into this situation came John Wesley, with a whole new dynamic built on personal commitment and faith supported by small groups as the building block of church. His focus was around people, not leaders. It was built around 'go' and not 'come,' and was led by John Wesley himself, who preached everywhere and anywhere. But this sense of momentum was also in his disciples, and was participative in the small groups. Everyone shared their trials, their tribulations, their temptations, and they encouraged one another in their faith. Their message was big. It was about the whole of life; it was about combating slavery, it was about how you treated your family, and being a good neighbour. They challenged one another to live the Christian life and because they primarily lived where they worked and worked where they lived, everybody knew each other. So the lives of these early Methodists had a big impact and in many of the poor communities which were ravaged by the effects of alcohol, they demonstrated the way a family could work. As families were discipled in small groups the workers' wages made it to the home, rather than being spent in the pub on the way. Because of this the families became well-nourished and were dressed properly. This was a spiritual revolution that brought about visible transformation and was changing England. Small groups were the heartbeat of this transforming work.

But do not just take my word for all this. Joel Comiskey, who has written widely on small groups, says the following:

> Wesley viewed preaching as the preamble to what would take place in the small groups. Discipleship took place in the lay-led class meetings through mutual ministry.

He follows this up by quoting a number of sources as follows:

> Henderson writes, 'The class meeting was the most influential instructional unit in Methodism and probably Wesley's greatest contribution to the technology of group experience.'[8] Although amazingly simple, it had a long-lasting impact that educators and religious leaders alike praised.
>
> A biography by Adam Clarke (who was a Methodist preacher during Wesley's lifetime) recounted Wesley's insistence about the priority of class meeting. 'From long experience I know the propriety of Mr Wesley's advice: "Establish class-meetings and form societies wherever you preach and have attentive hearers; for, wherever we have preached without doing so, the word has been like seed by the wayside"...Mr

Whitefield, when he separated from Mr Wesley, did not follow it. What was the consequence? The fruit of Mr Whitefield's labour died with himself. Mr Wesley's remains and multiplies.'[9] The class meetings were Wesley's strategy for making disciples, rather than hearing sermons.

Henry Ward Beecher said, 'The greatest thing John Wesley ever gave to the world is the Methodist class meeting.'

Dwight L Moody, nineteenth-century revivalist, said, 'The class meetings are the best institutions for training converts the world ever saw.'[10]

What we see from this Wesley model is two key things:

- Small groups were effective in discipling.
- Small groups mobilized people to make a difference.

Their influence was not only in terms of personal faith, but they began to deal with the big challenges of the day: slavery, poverty, class. It is said that John Wesley's Arminian theology created the middle classes, a sense that people could change and educate themselves. They were fundamental in starting the Sunday school movement, giving a role and place for women. It has been said that it was noted in one cabinet minute that there was concern that John Wesley had mobilized so many people that if he wanted to be prime minister, who could stop him!

People Power

Too many churches in the UK today look like the churches of the eighteenth century, where leaders do most of the work. The message is still 'Come on a Sunday' and the average church member is fairly passive. We need a new model. This new model is 'people power' supported and equipped by leaders. In these environments, every member is encouraged to be participative, to be missional, and to make a difference on their 'frontline'—a phrase developed by the London Institute of Contemporary Christianity.[11] It describes what we all do every day of our lives whether we are a business person, a stay-at-home person, go to school or college—we all have a frontline. This describes the relationships that we have with our neighbours, our colleagues, the parents at the school gate and all these natural everyday places where we find ourselves.

Small groups are the place where this heartbeat of mission is pumping which, enables transformation to happen.

There is another lesson to take away from John Wesley. If you read his substantive diaries and look at his extensive travel, you see something very interesting. He was challenging, equipping and encouraging the small group movement to continue. He knew this movement of small groups could not just be started up and left. In the UK I have seen a tendency for us to start small groups, but we have, in my view, underestimated the intentionality that is needed to keep them going. We need to keep on training leaders, providing support, to keep on motivating. This takes intention on the part of church leaders and their leadership teams. It means more time invested in the small group dimension of church life. It would be true, therefore, to say that if we want to embrace church in the big and small, it will mean a bit more work. However, the rewards are also greater as we see lives changed and our nation once again transformed as people are mobilized.

So, with that in mind, let us now look at some specifics as to what needs to be in place for successful, enduring small groups to be effective.

Trevor Withers

5 What Type of Small Group?

Inspired by the early church and by John Wesley, we move from the historical perspective to consider some of the foundational aspects of small groups that are important to have in place. I want to look at the beliefs and values that underpin the groups we are describing.

The small groups being proposed in this booklet are not just a pragmatic response to our current situation—they have an underlying set of beliefs and values that are driven by Scripture.

The Beliefs of Small Groups—the DNA

Let us start with the beliefs that will shape these groups. We can think of them as four strands of DNA, giving life to the atmosphere of the group.

The DNA strands are drawn from Mark 12.28, where Jesus lays out the most important commandment, saying, 'The most important one is this: "The Lord our God, the Lord is one. Love the Lord your God with all your heart and with all your soul and with all your mind and with all your strength." The second is this: "Love your neighbour as yourself." There is no commandment greater than these.'

Strand one carries the belief that God loves us and we want to know and follow him.

'The Lord our God is one.' He wants us to know what he is like, a God of love and relationship. He is good and invites us to love him with all our heart, mind and strength.

Strand two recognizes that God lives in community as Father, Son and Holy Spirit, and asks us to do the same.

It is God's dream that we love one another, and share community together, just as God does as Father, Son and Holy Spirit. Jesus said, 'By this all men will know that you are my disciples, if you have love for one another' (John 13.35). Therefore, when we listen to one another and take care of practical needs we are fulfilling God's dream, we are demonstrating real love.

We are also to love ourselves. It is also God's dream that each one of us would be whole. Sadly, however strong we are, we all carry some kind of collateral damage from life itself. When Jesus says we should love ourselves he is speaking about God's dream of wholeness. As we participate in a Christian community we should be healed and restored as individuals.

Strand three reminds us that like God, we are called to love a lost world as each one of us seeks to make a difference. We are told to, 'Love our neighbour,' those beyond our Christian community. To bring care and compassion to our needy world. It is our belief that this is what church should do and this is what small groups should do as part of the church—they empower us to love others.

Strand four is about participation and reminds us that these verses were written to everyone. Not just leaders or very special people, but all of us. It is you and I that are called to love God, to build community and to love a lost world. We are all called to participate in God's dream together.

The Values of Small Groups

A is for: All Involved

One of the secrets of the small group idea we are proposing is that it enables everyone in the group to participate actively. It is not just a case of hearing the leader's voice. Paul reminds us of this as he says, 'When you come together, each of you has a hymn, or a word of instruction, a revelation, a tongue or an interpretation' (1 Cor 14.26).

As we embrace the value of everyone involved, our small group gives us the perfect place in a safe environment for our faith to grow from passive to active. For us to begin to hear the sound of our own voice in a place where we can pray, a place where we can contribute, where we can experience God moving through us to encourage others—this can be truly life changing.

B is for: Becoming Disciples

Jesus says, 'My own sheep will hear my voice and I know each one, and they will follow me' (John 10.27). We know from this verse and many others that we are all called to be disciples, to be followers of Jesus who live out his values.

Small groups are places where discipleship can happen effectively. They create open and honest environments. Here we can be challenged and encouraged to grow in our faith and walk with God and others. We may find the courage to be honest, and ask for prayer, because at times we all find life difficult. It will be a place where we wrestle with Scripture together and understand how we can apply it to our lives. We will also experience the encouragement of others and the sense of togetherness. Being 'responsible to and for each other' is a powerful experience in helping us to grow, to change, and to live out the Christian life.[12]

C is for: Creating Community

We believe in a God who lives in community as Father, Son and Holy Spirit, and asks us to do the same. Our small groups are places where authentic Christian community can be nurtured.

> Jesus says, 'By this all men will know that you are my disciples, if you have love for one another' (John 13.35).

The love that we have for one another is not just of benefit to us—it is a demonstration to the world of the reality of the Christian message.

It is true to say that when we go to church on a Sunday there is a measure of community, but when we are in a small group we can step into a completely new level of community. What does this look like? In one group we had a lady suffering from chronic fatigue syndrome that meant, for a number of years, she had no energy. This was an opportunity for the small group community to cook meals and help support a family in crisis. At other times, it is even simpler things: a word, a phone call, a cup of coffee—those human connections that, in some way, carry the spirit of the divine God who himself lives in community as Father, Son and Holy Spirit.

D is for: Doing Evangelism

We are all called to be witnesses, to live out and share our faith with those around us.

Our small group can help us do this effectively in ways that are natural to us.

Jesus says, 'You are the salt of the earth, you are the light of the world' (Matt 5.13–14). In these two little phrases, Jesus is speaking to us about our mission. The sharing of our faith and making a difference where we work and live, this is our frontline and often feels challenging to us.[13] To help with this challenge LICC has produced a small group resource called *Fruitfulness on the Frontline.*

In small groups, we have an opportunity to help each other and, as we do this, we find that mission begins in the heart. It starts as a question: do we care about people? John 3.16 tells us that 'God so loved the world'; his motivation is love and that is why he sends his Son.

Therefore, we can pray that God will give us big hearts. A recent survey called *Talking Jesus* found that over 60% of people who come to faith are family members—or friends—of existing Christians.[14] In simple terms, doing evangelism is about being a good family member. It is about having unchurched friends. The role of the small group is to spend a few moments each week praying for the relationships we have, praying for one another to keep reaching out.

E is for: Encountering God

One of the great things about our Christian faith is that we believe in a God who reveals himself to us and wants to be known by us.

Whilst we often encounter God on our own, there is an added dimension to that encounter when we meet with others. We can have amazing encounters with God in our small group as he often speaks to us through each other.

In Acts 2.43, Luke gives us a wonderful description of how the early church encountered God in small groups. 'Everyone was filled with awe at the many wonders and signs performed by the apostles.' Jesus reminds us that 'Where two or three gather in my name, there am I with them' (Matt 18.20). Our encounter with God in small groups is different from our experience in larger settings; it is often more intimate and personal as we minister to one another. In this way we are transformed by his presence amongst us and the way he works through each of us.

So our small groups are built on four strands of DNA (the beliefs) and five values.[15]

Now let us explore how these beliefs and values are outworked in the leadership and structure of a small group.

Trevor Withers

6

Who Should Lead?

There is often a shortage of small group leaders in our churches. It is one of the main hurdles to starting new groups or even getting any groups running in the first place. Leading a small group does not have to be burdensome and, as the type of groups we are proposing here are highly participatory, leadership can be shared around the group through this participation.

If you just hear one voice, that of the leader, then the ownership of the group tends to be with the leader. However, if you hear many voices in a group, then the group feels as if it belongs to those in the group and is shared. This creates a greater level of engagement, ownership and involvement, making the leader's role much easier.

This chapter will demonstrate that leading a small group can be something that most people can do successfully, provided they have the right help and support.

One of the keys to developing more leaders is to offer a clear idea of what the groups will be like and what is involved in leading one. This sounds obvious to say, but in reality, leadership is sometimes seen as a mystical thing that you either have or do not have. This is not the case when it comes to leading small groups. Most people can pick up the skills that are required with some training. Like many things in life, developing small group leaders takes some intentionality. Inviting people to join a training group with the prospect of becoming better small group members—with the possibility of leading a group at some point in the future—is an initial step.

Developing small group leaders takes some intentionality

Cell UK have developed a simple-to-use resource called *Developing Leaders.*[16] This booklet enables both theoretical understanding and practical application in a real small group, with other potential group leaders from your church. Grounded in biblical beliefs and values, it includes reading material for people to learn on their own, questions for discussion in a group and material to be used in an actual small group setting, to see how it can all work in practice.

For groups to be truly participatory they need to have recognized rhythms and structures, which give a framework to the meeting time. This allows the meeting time to be divided up helpfully and gives movement, a fresh dynamic and impetus as the meeting progresses. Let us look at three reasons why I think these rhythms and structures are essential.

First, they make it possible to give different parts of the meeting to different people in the group. This delegation creates participation and ownership from the members of the group.

Secondly, they create safety as everyone knows the pattern they are following and feels safe making their contributions in the relevant places, rather than not being sure and becoming hesitant.

Thirdly, having a framework means that leadership of the group is easier as it becomes more of a facilitation style of leadership. The leader becomes the person who is linking the sections together and overseeing the flow, rather than the person who is contributing most. This means that leadership is open to more people and is less pressurizing.

A friend of mine thinks of these frameworks acting like a trellis in a garden. The trellis is there to support the growth of the plants; it is essential to help support the plants as they grow, but the trellis is not the focus, the plants are! In fact, the trellis is often completely covered by the plants.

The 4Ws for Small Groups

One of the most popular patterns that has been used by many groups for a number of years is the *4Ws*:

Welcome

This is an icebreaker, an open-ended question that all members would feel free to answer. Often the person asking the question will answer it first. Using this type of question gets everyone talking and creates an atmosphere of participation from the very start of the group.

Worship

In many groups this tends to be a creative, non-musical idea; perhaps a reflection from Scripture or a response to creation. This directs our attention towards God and creates a spiritual atmosphere in the group.

Word

This part of the small group meeting looks at Scripture in some way, often reflecting back on what was preached during the Sunday service. The group discuss the content of the message, look at the implications and applications in their lives and spend time in prayer and ministry together. This encourages God's word to be outworked in changed lives.

Witness

This will look at how group members are reaching out to their frontlines, being salt and light where they work and where they live. They might pray for one another in this context and think about their missional responsibility as individuals or as a small group with, perhaps, wider discussion on how they might support church-based initiatives.

The table below shows how this particular structure outworks the beliefs and values we have been looking at so far:

Structure	Belief	Value
Welcome	God loves and values us	All involved/creating community
Worship	Loving God	Encountering God
Word	Loving one another	Becoming disciples
Witness	Loving our lost world	Doing evangelism

In summary, we can see how using a framework or structure like the *4Ws* ensures that the beliefs and values at the heart of our church life can be consistently outworked through our small groups. It is key for both the well-being of the group and the individuals participating that those who lead each section as it is shared round each week are able to do it well. To help this happen, *Cell UK* has created a number of resources, including a set of 40 worship cards. These have creative worship ideas designed specifically for small groups and encouraging participation.[17] Similarly, there is a set of 40 missional ideas cards[18] and a booklet called *Help! I am leading part of my small group,* which gives practical tips and advice around each of the *4Ws* so people have a clear idea of what they are being asked to do.[19] See also *Small Groups: Big Mission* by Fusion,[20] and *The Spirit-filled Small Group* and *Lead: Guide a Small Group to Experience Christ* by Joel Comiskey.[21]

What Type of People Make Good Small Group Leaders?

I have been surprised by the variety of people who can lead a small group when it is based around the sort of rhythm I have just outlined. Many people end up leading because they have been part of a group and have enjoyed it so much that they want to create a new one themselves. Others have seen the way that the leadership feels shared, as different members pick up one of the sections and lead it. They feel that they can facilitate this type of group without it being as demanding as they may have thought. Many who lead find that they are simply one of two or three people in the group who share the practical leadership tasks. One will do the organizing, so they get other people to offer to lead a different part of the meeting each week. Another will run the WhatsApp group that many small groups use to keep in touch. Someone else organizes the more social get-togethers that the group enjoys from time to time. In this way, the named leader is supported and mainly facilitates the meeting times.

Most small-group leaders have a heart for people. Having said that, of course we should all, as Christians, have a heart for people as God does. It seems, however, that this comes more naturally to some than others. We are looking for people who are open to discovering how to facilitate a group who are good listeners as well as contributors.

It is also key that small groups and their leaders feel supported in their endeavours. Giving them a profile in the church and thanking them for their contribution to the life of the church are essential. Also, giving time to meet and encourage those leading groups and providing places for them to gather with others in leadership for encouragement and prayer is so valuable. This might happen every three months or so and provides a sense of belonging to a team as ideas are shared and encouragement given.

Another area of support for leaders of small groups is the need for support when there are challenging situations in their groups. We need to recognize that in some situations people need more support than the group can offer.

Where this is the case, a pathway needs to be in place so the small group leader can talk to a member of the central/relevant leadership team about their concerns. Each church will differ in response to these situations and have particular systems in place to enable discipleship and pastoral care, sometimes involving referral to an appropriate agency. The key here is to be clear about how this works and who needs to be involved. In most situations the earlier something is highlighted the better.

The way that these small groups differ from more historical forms of small group would be as follows:

- Light style of leadership which shows itself as lighter facilitating of the group; support by the group structure.
- The high level of shared participation from group members; a flexibility to put emphasis on different parts of the group meeting, depending on the needs of the group and relevant outreach.
- Creativity brought through people's contributions in leading each of the sections.
- An ability to follow the pathways of the members of the group into the broader world of work, local community and family life.

- Different models within the group.

In the next chapter Laurence celebrates what effect this all has on the individual, the church and the world around us.

7 Spiritual and Missional Outcomes

Laurence Singlehurst

Having looked at some of the foundational aspects and practicalities of running small groups, we now look at the outcomes of running small groups as we have described them.

We will look at these outcomes as they affect the individual personally, as well as the corporate outcomes that affect the wider life of the church, with all this leading to the effect that mobilized Christians can have on society.

Self-confidence

One of the things we have seen happen is the growing self-confidence of the individual member in the group. This happens through their participation and the encouragement and support of the other members of the group as they journey together. Perhaps the group starts with an icebreaker and the member hears their own voice and their contribution. They then might pray out loud for the first time and, week by week and month by month, as they participate their confidence grows. The little voices in their head that have said to them 'You can't do this' or 'You are no good at that' are silenced as they step out and, in the safety of the group, they have a go. I have seen people who have never thought of themselves as a spiritual leader take on a section of the meeting, maybe a ten-minute worship slot, using one of the worship cards mentioned earlier. Then they see how they can input into the lives of the other members and draw them into God's presence. Each time they lead a section they grow in confidence. I have seen individuals who join the group never having said a word in a corporate setting, yet within two years they are preaching on a Sunday morning.

Community

We all long to see a greater sense of community and practical outworking of Jesus' words, 'By this everyone will know that you are my disciples, if you love one another' (John 13.35). Through these small groups I have seen amazing community take place, showing itself in several ways. First, at an emotional level, during an icebreaker (which is often in the form of a question which each member of the group answers), you might share some personal details about yourself. There are also opportunities for members to share practical or spiritual needs with other members for prayer and this openness causes what some psychologists call bonding. This shared information creates an emotional response, a sense of acceptance and community. Secondly, this community grows when members have a need. For example, someone is sick, and members help by cooking a meal or caring for a child, whatever the case may be. Thirdly, members grow in confidence as they use the spiritual gifts that God has given them in the group. They might have a spiritual word of encouragement for another member, or a picture that God gives them to share. This often happens as needs are shared in response to looking at Scripture together in the word section, and members of the group gather round to pray for the one in need. Therefore, through each of these three areas community grows at an emotional level, a practical level and a spiritual level.

Discipleship

We are all called to make disciples. Our experience of these small groups is that greater discipleship just happens, and it happens in this way: in a segment of the small group meeting there will be content from the Bible, perhaps looking at what was preached or taught on a Sunday, perhaps looking at a video or some other form of input. At the end of this input the person leading that segment does not necessarily look to what people have understood in a head-knowledge way, although that might be important; they look to what the application is of what they have heard, asking, 'How does this affect you as a Christian?' 'How does it affect your personal walk with God?' 'How does it affect your relationship with others?' Then prayer is offered, if people want it, based on helping each other apply to our lives what we have been looking at together. Going back to our historical model, John Wesley was very keen on application and used powerful questions to see it happen: 'How does this make you different? A better husband, a better disciple, a better witness?' So, discipleship is enabled as application takes place within the supportive and accountable framework of the small group, and powerful transformation can occur as the group journeys together.

Missional Purpose

Missional purpose is like the holy grail of small groups and, perhaps, the holy grail of church. How do we help people to be truly missional? I think the kinds of small groups we have discussed have helped to find this holy grail. Let me take a moment to share why I think this is the case. Fifteen or so minutes is put aside at the end of the meeting to think of an individual's frontline, whether that be in business, at home, at school or college—and the relationships that we have with our neighbours, our colleagues, the parents at the school gate and all these natural everyday places where we find ourselves. These fifteen minutes of focus each week will look very varied. It might be about how we pray for these environments; it might be how we pray for ourselves, and we ask God for a bigger heart so that we might care for people and reach out to them. It might be encouragement to be hospitable and how we build relationships and friendships, what we say and what we do not say. As you can imagine these fifteen minutes every week add up over the course of a year to a great deal of mission-focused time. This time each week, drip by drip, drop by drop, fills the reservoirs of our group members' missional capacity. We know from research that the people close to us are the ones most likely to take a journey of faith so as members of the small group are encouraged to develop these relationships, in getting to know more people the overall witness of the church is multiplying and growing. To use a metaphor, we are, as a whole church, holding a lot more hands and the love of Jesus is reaching out through our church in a greater way. This is enabled through the support and encouragement of small groups.

Corporate Outcomes

We have looked at four personal outcomes. There are also three corporate outcomes I have seen over the years while working with churches. First, as people grow in confidence and discipleship within the context of the small group, they inevitably begin to take more responsibility in the wider and bigger groups, such as church on Sunday and leadership teams.

As the church develops its rhythm of mission with events around Christmas, meetings at Easter and guest services, through fun events over the summer and, maybe, *Alpha* in the autumn, members who have been developing projects and relationships inspired by the small group can now invite people into the corporate functions and mission of the central church. So now we see a missional partnership between the small group and the main church. These first two outcomes that we have described will have a major positive impact on the wider church; there will be more mature members who are eager to volunteer and to be at the core of church life and more working together. But there is more.

Thirdly, and in some ways most excitingly, the church is acting as a catalyst to see the kingdom of God come, not just within its own walls and activities, but through the lives of its members on their frontlines. The reach of the church is dramatically increased in this way. Every member becomes a kingdom carrier wherever they are, bringing transformation as they live their lives for Jesus, demonstrating his values.

So, how do we begin? If you have never run small groups in your church the best way forward is to start a test or prototype group. Here, one of the church leaders would gather six to eight people, choose a small group system that they think might work for them and, for a period of time (perhaps six to twelve weeks), run a small group. *Cell UK* provides a resource to help this called *Developing Leaders*, which would give the members of this test group some reading material to work through. It gives them three chapters to read, three chapters to discuss in the group before running a small group based on the material in the last three chapters. This can be evaluated by those who have taken part and by the church leaders, and then it could be rolled out slowly. It is never a very good idea to just announce a small group system and impose it on the church. It is best to test an idea with several groups of people, and when you have some confidence in it slowly begin to invite other members of the church into that experience.

In this booklet we have reflected on today's culture in the UK, on some of the challenges facing the church now and in the future, and what we can learn from other small group pioneers in history.

What seems clear is that we must strengthen the individual church members in their role, to be active disciples and to make a difference. Small groups can help to do this: the members develop their spiritual life and outreach supported by their small group, and affect the world around them.

Let us continue to give focus and leadership energy to the place of small groups in our churches as we move forward. I would encourage us to think, strategize and plan in both the large corporate setting and in the small group setting. When these two work together the heart of our churches will pump well and bring life to many. The challenge is for each church to think through how they can do small groups, reinvigorate existing groups and start new ones so that these positive outcomes are at the very heart of our church life together.

Notes

1 See www.churchofengland.org/millions-join-worship-online March 2021.

2 'Our streets are not empty but filled with love', *The Times,* May 2020.

3 S Murray, *Post Christendom* (Milton Keynes: Paternoster Press, 2004) p 20.

4 N Spencer, *Beyond Belief* (London: The London Institute for Contemporary Christianity, 2006) p 3.

5 L Singlehurst, *The Gospel Message Today* (Grove Evangelism booklet Ev100).

6 'Talking Jesus' research 2015: talkingjesus.org

7 K Harrison, Director, Faith Research Centre. Com Res June 2018.

8 J Comiskey, *2000 Years of Small Groups: A History of Cell Ministry in the Church* (Moreno Valley, CA: CCS Publishing, Kindle Edition, 2014) Kindle Location 2079-2081.

9 *ibid*, Kindle Location 2084–2087.

10 *ibid*, Kindle Location 2088–2091.

11 https://licc.org.uk/

12 W Beckham, Cell training material (Houston, TX: Touch Ministries, 2003).

13 M Greene: https://licc.org.uk/ourresources/lifeonthefrontline

14 'Talking Jesus' research (Ventura, CA: Barna Group, 2015) p 23.

15 P Potter, *The Challenge of Cell Church* (Abingdon: BRF, 2001).

16 L Singlehurst and T Withers, *Developing Leaders* (Cell UK 2018): https://celluk.org.uk/product/developing-leaders-training-for-small-group-leaders

17 https://celluk.org.uk/product/40-creative-worship-ideas-small-groups/

18 https://celluk.org.uk/product/40-missional-ideas-for-small-groups/

19 https://celluk.org.uk/product/help-leading-part-of-my-small-group/

20 https://www.fusionmovement.org

21 https://joelcomiskeygroup.com